AF439318

You are Seen
You are Heard
You are Loved

Akeem Lloyd

ISBN 979-8-9857159-1-0 (Paperback Edition)
ISBN 979-8-9857159-0-3 (Hardcover Edition)
ISBN 979-8-9857159-2-7 (E-Book)

Editing by Careen Lawrence
Book Design by Maria Doumpa

Printed in the United States of America. First Printing February 2022

AkeemSpeaks, LLC
P.O. Box 29163
Providence, RI 02909

I'm struggling with depression, accepting myself, opening up and being the best me that I can be. I'm struggling with coming to terms with my emotions. I feel like I haven't been able to take care of myself, and I haven't been able to learn how to love myself. Opening up is such a challenge for me because I hate feeling vulnerable, especially to other people. I'm always wanting to do the right thing but I feel like I'm always pushing myself too hard while asking myself if what I am doing is enough or if I'm ever going to be enough. I'm always telling myself I'm going to be alright but I am not sure if I'm just lying.

-College Freshman

Paintbrushes
An original poem by Akeem Lloyd

Thursday, March 14th, I sat in a classroom filled with Scientists, Artists, Entrepreneurs, Congressmen and Women. I sat in a class filled with 33 Paintbrushes, ready to paint the world with Ambitious Colors. Their canvas, their Canvas, is as big as their thoughts, and I am simply there to help them choose their colors.

They will never be Picasso, but they can be better, and everyday I strive to bring out the best artist in them; the best in them. They have yet to see what their paint can do. It's only a matter of time before their best will come, and I pity the fool who chooses to disagree.

Our kids are Intellectual Time Bombs waiting to explode and I pray, I pray that I'm there when their confidence goes boom, kaboom, bam, and they start to break down every stereotype that has ever labeled them as felons, criminals, and convicts, and they start to break down every stereotype that has gotten them killed. Trayvon Martin. Tamir Rice. Breonna Taylor. Roxanne Moore. For every stereotype that has ever gotten them beaten- Sandra Bland- and placed behind bars. My students will paint themselves into history. Never forgetting their history, they will use pastel colors because it looks better in the sun, yea, brighter in the sun.

Their lives will reflect the hard Work of Martin Luther King. Their passion will bounce off walls and into their communities like Malcolm X. Their determination will look a little more like Harriet Tubman. They, I, we, can change this world one paint stroke at a time. I serve because Frederick Douglass once said "once you learn how to read, you will be forever free" and "it's easier to build strong children than it is to repair broken men".

My students will learn not to bend. I serve because they have built more prisons, I serve because they are building more prisons, and I refuse to watch as it grows when I know that we can be a part of its downfall.

I am not asking for your sympathy. I am asking that you care more. Although they may not greet you with a smile, inside, a hi is all that they care for. You'll be surprised by the number of artists you meet every day.

I serve students who, like me, find it hard to believe in themselves, who find it hard to see themselves. I serve students who find it hard just to be themselves. We are blueprints for positivity. I am a believer in the power of our youth, the bridge our children can believe is stabled. I am the voice that reminds them how great they are, and we can be the voices that reminds them how great they are. I am merely a Paintbrush. I am the Journal they can write in, the shoulder they can lean on, I am just a mentor who cares.

I serve with a purpose, for a purpose, to instill self-love and self-worth in our youth. So when you ask me why I serve and I simply respond,because I have to, please do not feel offended by my short answer. Sometimes it's hard to relay these words that mean so much to my identity. I identify with students whose parents have been addicted to drugs. I serve students whose parents have been deported,  or are too busy to care. I serve because someone told me I matter.

Thursday, March 14th, I sat in a classroom filled with Scientists

Artists, Entrepreneurs, Congressmen and Women. I sat in a Classroom filled with 33 Eighth graders, ready to paint this world with Ambitious Colors. They may never be Picasso, but they can be better. I am because someone told me I Matter, and that greatness is a Mindset. I serve because, who will tell them?

To The Youth

To every young person I have ever had the opportunity to meet, support, mentor, teach, and listen to, THANK YOU for allowing me to be a part of your journey. Whether it was for a season, in the moment, or for a number of years, my love for you will never waver. I am forever grateful, forever honored, and forever privileged to have had your trust, your belief, and the time you spent alongside my journey. I did not then, and will not ever take for granted the experiences we all shared.

From the Boys and Girls Club of Atlantic City, to the very first Educational Opportunity Fund (EOF) class I supported in Camden, New Jersey, to the middle schools in Philly, the Educational Opportunity Fund Programs throughout the Garden State of NJ, to the high schools in Los Angeles, Toronto, South Africa, Ghana, Kenya, and Providence Rhode Island, every state or country I have had this distinguished opportunity to serve young people, thank you.

You all have shown me something that I will never forget; Love. You all have given me something that I will never forget; hope. Thank you for leaving your footprints on my heart. I pray you all receive years of good health, wealth, prosperity, and an abundance of joy. I see you, I hear you, and I love you.

I Am, Because You Are.

<u>To The Parents and Guardians</u>

To every parent and guardian who has ever trusted me with their child, and believed in the commitment I made to you and them, THANK YOU. To every teacher, school official, EOF/TRiO/Upward Program that has ever contracted me to come in, THANK YOU. I pray that I lived up to the commitment I made to you and your students.

<u>To my Family, Loved Ones and Mentors</u>

To my family, and loved ones, mentors and everyone who has ever poured into me, to list you all by name would be a whole book in itself; please know that you all mean a lot to me, I am who I am today because of the lessons you all have given me. THANK YOU for believing me, holding me accountable, encouraging me, and helping me feel seen, heard and loved.

<u>Trigger Warning</u>

This book has questions that can or may bring back past experiences or thoughts, please center yourself, and or make sure that you can identify where your support systems/people are. Feel free to put the book down and come back to it. Feel free to skip the next page. Take care of yourself first.

I would be remiss, if, as an artist, I did not share the reality of what young people have and are still experiencing. In order to support them, we have to know, understand and be willing to hear what is not pretty. To think, how disturbing these questions are to us as the readers, consider how damaging it is for those who are the ones feeling and asking themselves these questions.

Do you know what it is like to feel lonely as a child? Raise your hand if you do; nod your head slowly? Did you have anyone you could turn to during those times as a child? If not, did you wish you had someone, or would you have liked to have had someone there to turn to?

If you did, how did that person make you feel? From what you can recall, what characteristics did they have which helped you feel safe, secure, seen, heard, and or loved?

Unfortunately, there is a young person somewhere in the world, in the same community as you, who does not feel as though they have someone like the someone who supported you.

Have you ever wondered why a child is so quiet?

I will ask you what a student asked me. "Do you know what it is like to wake up in the morning wishing that you never did, and to go to bed at night wishing that you won't wake up?" (2021)

# I Don't Blame Anyone

I first started working with youth because it was just a job, something I could do while in high school to make some money. I was a peer mentor at the Boys and Girls Club of Atlantic City. I worked Monday through Friday, and every summer. During the school year I helped 3rd through 5th graders with their homework. Encouraging them to believe in themselves is what I remember the most. The job was one that I was excited to do, but the intentions I have today are not the same as when I first started out. I mean, I was 14, I didn't know anything about these three actions; youth development, the process of healing, and self-love. I couldn't talk about the importance of them as I can talk about it now. I was young, hell, I needed all three of those actions myself, just like I needed someone to see me, hear me, and to love me.

As time ticked, and life transformed, so did I, and so did my reasons for working with youth. It was no longer just a job to me, it became clear that it was my social responsibility to do this work. Some may define it  as a calling, and others will define it as purpose. Maybe my social responsibility and purpose can equally work together in parallel, but I wouldn't say that working with youth is my purpose. The action of working with youth, I tend to believe, is a bridge; the bridge to my purpose, and the vessel in me is being leveraged in this youth space to do something greater than myself. I am still learning what that is.

I grew up in a silent household where we never spoke about our feelings. We didn't talk about our emotions. We didn't talk about love. I never heard the words 'I love you' growing up in my household. No one gave me a hug growing up in my household. Between the ages 5 to 17, I was already learning what it meant to wear the mask. I blame no one for it.

I was raised by my grandparents in Atlantic City, New Jersey, home. Alongside me was my older brother, I was the youngest, while my oldest brother was still living in Brooklyn, New York. In my household, expressions of love were not the norm, and to say the 'norm' is to acknowledge that it was present, when the truth is, it wasn't. Now in my heart of hearts, I truly believe that my grandparents did everything they could with everything they had; I believe my grandparents loved me like they knew how to love.

I am older now, so my understanding of love is different, my understanding of how they loved me has grown, and my understanding of how they were taught to love makes it all make sense. But, back then I was too young to know. As a little boy my youth development needed more. One may say, but Keem they fed you, they clothed you, how could you say or think something like that, and I would simply respond, just like someone can be in a room full of people, and friends and still feel alone. The physical presence of someone next to you does not mean they are emotionally present while being next to you.

Just because I had food on my plate, and clothes on my back does not mean or equal to me feeling loved. There are a lot of young people who would agree with that.

Everyone has certain and specific needs, those needs play a huge role in the psychological and emotional development in a person. Those needs, when met, serve as a security blanket. The psychological and emotional comfort one has, is directly correlated to the levels in which a young person feels socially comfortable. When these needs are met, it triggers neurons and releases serotonin that activates a sense of calm and safety, i.e. relaxation. Education and science teaches us, when a child feels safe; when a child feels comfortable; when a child is more relaxed, they are better prepared to learn. They are readily able to receive information better. If educators and scientists have not figured that out as yet, we are failing our kids, and we are not supporting their learning needs. If those needs are not met, that young person runs the risk of falling into the cycle of feeling unloved, unsafe, and emotionally distant from themselves and others. The psychological effects are; survival mode or hopelessness and helplessness. The battle between the two determines if a child or young person chooses to keep going, or chooses to give up.

Yes, on the outside, my hierarchy of needs were being met, without a doubt, G-Money and my Granddad provided everything they could, exactly how they knew how. Everything except the thing that was missing. I didn't understand what that missing thing was though until I got to college. All of my needs were not met growing up, it is my reality, I don't blame anyone, but the result of that left me feeling emotionally hurt and isolated; psychologically isolated and alone, and to top it off, there were other factors that were outside of my grandparents control that left me feeling like a social outcast. When you add up all of these factors, there is a reason why I didn't feel seen, didn't feel heard, and didn't feel loved.

Growing up with older siblings makes you the youngest right, and one would think because you are the youngest you would get all, or, most of the attention. That wasn't the case for me. My brother was smart, and he got excellent grades. He did things by the book, never really got in trouble at school, and would always receive high praise from the teachers. I, on the other hand, had my moments of genius, but had too many moments of doing the wrong thing. I wasn't into school as much as my brother was. I was actually the total opposite of him. For a long time we dressed differently, acted differently, we were into different out of school interests such as sports and what our friends wanted to do for fun. Because of our differences, personally, I felt like an outsider in my own home.

**I see you, because I don't know the last time you felt seen.**

Truth is, the essence of this book carries the stories of my personal life, captures the transformation of who I was, what I felt and experienced, while taking the real lived experiences of young people with whom I have had the privilege to work with, support, mentor, and reiterating to young people all over the world, I see you, I hear you, and I love you. Big emphasis on the I Love You.

My mentor and big brother Jeff Joseph once told me, "Keem, speak your truth, only you can do that, and when you do nobody can take that away from you." I am a firm believer that stories serve as an inspiration to others, and you don't need to be an athlete, a celebrity, a millionaire, or a global icon to have your story serve as an inspiration for someone who needs it. You just have to be willing and open to sharing it.

As young as 5 years old, I was very observant. Call it a gift, maybe. It was something that came naturally, but also as a response to my learning curve. I remember being in the school yard watching the older kids play when I had to stand in line. There were opportunities where us littler kids could run around, too, but the big kids took up most of the school yard. I watched how some kids had their parents with them, either standing in line next to them or on the other side of the fence waiting for the teacher to come pick them up. I didn't have that. I didn't even know where my parents were, but something inside me wanted that. The visual of seeing others hold hands with their folx, seeing father and son, mother and daughter, family member and child having a bonding moment, I wanted that. G-Money couldn't always walk us to school and she didn't have to, with my older brother being old enough, and the school only being but a couple blocks away, she trusted him. Being on that playground as a 5 year old though, seeing what I saw, there was a level of visibility those kids were getting, that I wondered why I wasn't. Their folx were there to SEE them off to school, and into class, where were mine?

Between the 1st grade and 5th grade, everything became a norm. My dad was inconsistent, and my mom came down once a month for a couple hours. G-Money was raising my brother and I, taking care of my grandfather who was blind, and now had the responsibility of mothering two little girls who were my baby sisters. I'm older now, I can respectfully acknowledge that that was a lot on her shoulders. The younger me was too young to know. Now I am the middle child, and "old enough" to do things on my own. That is exactly how I felt, on my own.

Story time, I had a student that I worked with and mentored while I was working in Philly. She was experiencing some things that I don't believe any young person should ever have to experience. On the outside, she reminded me of me, she was all smiles, and showed signs of joy on a daily basis. She was a leader. I don't think she knew how strong of a leader she was, but her personality was big, and she was smart. She wasn't in my grade or cohort of students that I worked with directly, but I had stairwell duty during the time she had lunch. Every day she would walk by me, and we would exchange friendly greetings. Oftentimes, she would come to the bottom of the steps during her lunch period to talk. I would be sitting about halfway up, somewhere in the middle of this dark blue painted cornerstone of the school, and we would talk most of the period. We would talk about her dreams, her goals, and what she wanted to accomplish. We would do this every day. Well, we would do it every day except for the days she wasn't there. I started noticing the moments when she was gone, especially the moments where she was gone for long periods of time.

Whenever she would come back, we would pick right back up where we left off. But I always made sure that I acknowledged her absence. "Hey how are you doing, I haven't seen you in a while". "Heyyy, where have you been?". I was in my 20s, so this type of communication was normal to me. She was experiencing some things that I don't believe any young person should have to experience. On the inside, she reminded me of me. Slowly but surely she started to share more, more of what she was feeling, and how the loneliness and depression of it all was weighing heavy on her. All the things I too was familiar with, myself. She had family at home, friends at the school, leadership opportunities in her lap. She was all smiles, and showed signs of joy on a daily basis. But deep down inside she was hurting, a feeling that too many young people feel on a daily basis. One day she came back after being absent for a really long time, and I noticed the hospital band on her wrist. I asked, "are you okay". This came after our initial positive greeting, and a handful of jokes. I am pretty sure we both needed a laugh, until nothing was funny anymore. When I asked her are you okay, I was not expecting the response she gave. "I was in the hospital, I tried to kill myself."

The dark blue stairwell suddenly became all black, and the world started to slow down, she was no longer looking up, and I was no longer looking down. My heart. This young girl was so young. Too young to be practicing such a practice. Too bright to be part-taking in such actions, but there we were. It's a feeling that too many young people feel, and a practice that too many young people practice. I was hurt, my eyes went from staring at cracks of paint on the wall, to the heavy grey door behind her, to finally back at her. My heart. The silence that filled that empty stairwell felt like forever. I thought of so many things to say. What do you say? I began to say what my heart felt. I told her, "I see you". I told her what I thought of her future, and reminded her of all the dreams and goals that she wanted to accomplish. I reminded her that she has a friend in me, how I look forward to speaking with her during lunch, and that I cared about her well-being. "Life is hard, but you can't accomplish your goals if you don't give yourself a chance". And then I reminded her one more time before the bell sounded, "I see you".

Not everyone ends up being as strong as she was, and still is. The suicide numbers **prove** it. Not everyone who felt or feels the way she did had someone to see them. I don't know if the gesture of making it known, that you see a young person, would stop that young person from practicing self-harm, but I do believe with all my heart that it could help, or at least have a big enough impact on that young person to have them second guess it.

The thing is, there are a lot of stories like hers, unfortunately; there is probably a young person right now who is reading this book who feels like she did; the same way I did; alone, depressed, unloved, with low self-esteem and questioning life. If this is you, please know that you are not alone, please know that you too have a life to live, to enjoy, to experience the beauty of breathing and doing things you have always dreamed of. You too are strong enough to keep going. You too are brave enough to keep going. Fight back. You too have a reason to fight back, because when this book is old and outdated, your story, yes you, your story is going to be the reason why another young person much younger than you, will also choose to fight back.

I am happy to say the story of the student I just shared is an inspiration, she fought back, so much so that she graduated from High School and went off to College. She is still all smiles, she is still a leader, and I am still proud of her. I recently spoke to her actually, and during our catching up we spoke about those times during that period of her life, to celebrate her, her perseverance, and everything she has accomplished. She told me, I didn't know how to talk about it, so I did things in school hoping that someone would ask me about what was going on and how I felt, hoping that someone would ask me how I was really doing. But no one did. I just wanted to be seen.

When she said that, I felt it. It reminded me of when I started to get bullied in the 3rd grade. I was kind of tall for my age, I had long arms, so I could have passed for a 4th grader and maybe even a young 5th grader. The bullying began when I started walking home by myself. The path home was a straight arrow, you couldn't get lost, it was pretty much out in the open, and up until the 3rd grade it was pretty safe. In the city we have what is called the 1st village, the 2nd village, and the 3rd village. I had family who lived in the 3rd. When I started walking home by myself I would walk on the street that the 1st village sat on. It was routine at this point, until one day these two brothers started bothering me. I will never forget these moments, because trauma recovery isn't linear, although I have learned to manage the moments when I recall them.

It was nice out, the sun was booming, I was wearing this colorful snapback hat, t-shirt, jeans and sneaks. On the opposite side of the street I was walking on, was what I considered a park. It was a dirt lot, there was a sign in the middle of it, It was wide open so you could clearly see what was happening on the other side, as well as on the side I was walking on.

There were always old heads with brown paper bags and bottles filled with yesterday's dreams out there chilling. I paid them no mind, and I am pretty sure they returned the favor. As I walked I noticed two boys sitting on their stoop. I didn't think anything of it, so I kept it pushing. I didn't wave hi, or look their way because we didn't do things like that. A couple steps after I had already passed them on the stoop, I heard them talking and before I knew it, one ran in front of me and the other stood behind me.

They started punching me and shoving me, pulling on my book-bag and using it to spin me around. I was scared as hell. I was caught off guard by how fast they ran up on me, and even more caught off guard that I was actually being physically attacked for no reason. When I finally broke free, I ran home.

When I got home, I proceeded as if everything was just fine. As I shared earlier, I grew up in a pretty silent house, so expressing myself wasn't something I learned to do; I felt comfortable doing, or knew how to do. I kept day one to myself, went to bed, woke up, went to school and got chased home again. I kept day two to myself. This happened every day, and every day I would act as if everything was okay. I would come home, eat, sleep, and go back to school. Most times my grandparents were home when I got back from school, but when my grandparents weren't home, I had to go across the street to the community center for a couple hours until they got back. I would go to the Police Athletic League building pretty much every day. We called it P.A.L. for short, I would go there ready to be a kid, play sports, have fun, you know, do what little kids do. But the P.A.L building also became a safe haven for me, a place where I was able to go to be free. I didn't have to think about being bullied, punched on, chased, and any of the other inner thoughts I was having, feeling alone, sad, why is this happening to me. Basketball was always my go to. The P.A.L building had some nice courts there. The floor was made up of blue rubber like material. The ceilings were so high. On the same floor as the court, there was a pool table, video games, and a space where homework help was given. On the floor above that, there was a whole boxing ring, and weights everywhere. It was always hot, humid and had a funny rubber smell to it. The basketball court became my home away from home, and the P.A.L building provided that.

When the thoughts and emotions of hopelessness and helplessness begin to consume one's thoughts and how they begin to behave, it impacts how we interact with the world. We begin to live a double entendre life where we don't want to be seen, we are scared to be seen in this state that we are in, and on the other hand, we want to be seen, we want someone to care about us and how we are really doing. We know when to give a little, and we know when to give just enough, all in the name of safety. From a very young age we are taught to be strong, to not let anyone see you cry; to never let anyone know you're hurt; because you never want to give someone that kind of power and influence over you. "You never want them to use that against you" is what I used to hear. Nowadays I think about how the impact of slavery and Jiim Crow serves as triggers to this ideology that continues to be passed down from one black generation to the next. If they didn't use torture and fear tactics to scare my people, it makes me wonder what would be different. To add to that idea of having to be strong, I was a black boy growing up in the city, my grandparents just wanted to make sure that I came home every night.

In our communities, it was about protecting yourself, and protecting your feelings is a big lesson taught throughout. The idea of it comes with good intentions, and I honestly understand why, because it can get rough out there, unfortunately. This is the beginning of young people learning where and how to wear the mask. I get it, but the problem is, young people are taught to be so strong, and in many ways, reserved, that it creates this hardened interior and exterior, without ever teaching the power of vulnerability.

One may argue to say, we needed that hard toughness to get through it all, and look how I still turned out, living my best life. To that I would say, awesome, I feel you, but how many brothers and sisters didn't? How many brothers and sisters experienced trauma and could never get over that part of their lives? How many brothers and sisters are still hardened, and struggling to interact with the world in a healthy way, a healthy relationship or friendship because we never addressed it? I get why we have to be tough, have to be strong, and why we have to wear the mask, but being 33 years old now and a survivor of my own self-harm, I also have the right to question why. More importantly, why can't we develop and implement a healthier balance of toughness when needed, and mental and emotional health support along the way.

Just like that, I too was wearing the mask. The bullying never stopped that year, and it only got worse. At one point, I made the decision to start running before I got to their stoop, just so that I could have a head start. When they didn't catch me right in front of their place, they would chase me for another two blocks before finally deciding to let me be. I never looked back during those Olympic sprints, because I knew if I made it past the pink colored building, Liberty apartments on Baltic Avenue, I was almost free, because the light on New York Avenue is where I lived.

One day, they caught me before I could get past them. If they caught me in front of their crib, it was easier for them to do more to me because there was a gap between their building and the building next to it. In this gap, between the two brown bricked buildings, you could turn the corner and be out of sight. On this day, I remember them pushing me into that little area and forcing me to lay down on this dirty ass mattress. No one was around, or in plain sight. They pushed me down, one held me while the other began to fold the mattress. When they rolled me up, they picked up the mattress and threw me into the dumpster that was right next to where we were. When I looked up, one of them pulled a gun out, pointed it at me and said "I dare you to move". They closed the lid. I sat in that dumpster for hours. Scared. I didn't know if they were still out there, being quiet on purpose, but as much as I was scared of them and the unknown of potentially getting shot, killed, who knows what, I was more scared of G-Money. There was a time frame that she expected me to be home. I already knew I was going to be in trouble for being late, but I couldn't fathom what she would have done if I waited any longer. I lifted the black lid, and when I didn't see them I jumped out of that green dusty dumpster and ran home. When G-money answered the door she asked, "where were you", and the only answer I could think of was, I was outside playing. Like many young people do today, in an effort to be strong, to be safe, I put the mask on.

I kept all 1,095 total days to myself. Not once did I tell G-Money, my Granddad, my brother, family, teachers or coaches that I was being bullied, chased home or that I had been thrown into a dumpster. How was I supposed to tell my Grandma that I was staring at the barrel of a gun? I was only in 3rd grade. They bullied me for three years straight.

I became angry. I was mad at everything. Internally I was fuming. Why did they do this to me? What did I ever do to them? What made them start, what made them stop? I had questions for days, and no way to get answers. I found myself doing what a lot of young people do today, I walked around with bottled up emotions for years to come. I let it fester, and would verbally express it through temper tantrums, through jokes where I tried to be the class clown and or defiance. I was still very respectful for the most part, but 3rd grade through 7th grade, I experienced my first F, my first C's and D's. I was getting calls home, sitting under desks, displayed acts of violence, had my first fights, and ultimately stopped caring about school overall. Like the student I worked with, like too many young people do today, we swallow our feelings, and put distance between us and those around us to protect ourselves.

There is a student I worked with, his mom had just signed him up to be a part of my after school youth program. He was a Middle School student. Whether he wanted to participate or not, he showed up at our first meeting. I introduced myself, told them all that I was here to support them and their growth. I rattled off a bunch of reasons why I believe in them, and how excited I was to get to know them. I don't think he blinked the whole time. He was soft spoken, when he said his name, he didn't say it with much confidence. I mean, how can I blame him, he was in a room with other students he didn't know like that, they didn't know him like that, and he still didn't know me so I get it. The analysis was already made though, this young man had his guard up, and I was going to have to work for his trust if I wanted to build a relationship with him.

Every time I saw him in the hallway I would say "what's up", just to let him know that I saw him. I may have even come off as annoying that year, but I needed him to know that I saw him. Just like so many youths today, he kept his guard up, had very little to say, and when I asked him how he was doing he would always respond "I'm good". I learned the importance of consistency through the mentorship of someone who was very consistent with me. It was the first lesson of youth development that I learned, not taught, but learned. As much as this student tried to maintain his security and tough demeanor, I remained steadfast and consistent. I challenged him when he was with us after school. I used loving actions such as daps and hugs to remind him that I was here, and that I saw him. As time went on, I began to learn about his situation. He was being raised by his mom, his dad wasn't really providing what this young man needed, and his absence in the home didn't make it any better. This young man was angry inside, and he did everything to hold that anger in. He was hurt but was afraid to show it, afraid to talk about it, and afraid to let it be known.

He was essentially the man of the house, heightening his expectations and responsibilities. There are young people across the world, not just the US, who have heightened expectations and responsibilities at a young age. This was not new to me, but as I learned more about him, the clearer it became. He was an older brother, his younger brother needed a lot of attention. I get it, this brother wanted to be seen, and so I did what Mr. Justin did for me. I saw him for him, and loved on him like I knew how; I stayed consistent. Our relationship got stronger, he began to communicate more, took more initiative. I watched him grow up some. There were still some moments where he had to check his anger, but like I said, trauma recovery isn't linear.

## Plant the Seed, Water the Seed, Support it as it Grows

Who is Mr. Justin? Mr. Justin showed me what consistency looked like, and ultimately what it felt like. When I moved from New York Avenue to North Carolina Avenue, I stopped going to the P.A.L building because the Boys & Girls Club of Atlantic City (BGC) was closer now. I remember when I first walked in, I was a High School freshman, so I didn't need a guardian to sign me up to be a member. I did it myself. I got a tour of the building, and afterwards they said I could stay just to hangout, and so I did. It was colorful on the inside, bright colors everywhere. When you first walked in, the gym was to the left, a help desk was right in front of you, and to the right was everything else. They had a kitchen for snack time, an upstairs for activities, lounging, and homework help. On the first floor, the club had a ping pong table and a gaming system. There was this game, I still don't know what it is called, but it was fun and I played it a lot. The object of the game was to line your balls up anywhere on your side of the field, anywhere where you thought it would make it hard for the opponent to knock your balls in the hole. Once you set up the field, one player had a white ball, and would roll it to your side trying to knock all your balls in before you did theirs. That game was a member favorite.

As I was standing in the welcome desk area, a man with cornrows was walking through, light skin, pale even, wearing some sweats, a t-shirt and some kicks that would respectfully fall under the 'WHAT ARE THOSE' category. He asked me my name, and in a soft voice I told him, he introduced himself as Mr. Justin. He welcomed me to the club, and then went into the gym. I left. The next day when I returned to the BGC, Mr. Justin was there to greet me. He said what's up and asked me if I was good. I said yeah and kept it pushing. The next day, Mr. Justin greeted me and asked me if I was good, "what's up Keem? You good?". Once again I told him yeah and moved along. Similar to the student I just shared, I was him, he was me. I did my best to keep Mr. Justin at a distance, I kept my guard up because it was the only way I knew how to protect myself.

I didn't just wear the mask; I wore it well, like many young people today. My armor was behind every "I'm good" lie I ever told. I wore it with pride, knowing that many people would never really question if I was really good or not. Everyone took it for face value, and to this day, we still take it for face value.

We've been taught to respond that way, both the person who asks the question, and the person who responds with I'm good. The person who asks the question, out of respect, mutual love and or a level of friendship, will ask, and accepts the answer as final. We are taught to mind our business, and if someone had something to say, they would say it. We are also taught not to say it, even if we weren't good in that moment; it became so natural to respond that way. When in reality, the truth is, everyone isn't always good, and asking them again, "how are you, really? or "how are you really doing?" may ignite an honest response from the person you are asking because, one, asking it that way does come off as a certain level of healthy concern, and, two, by adding "really" into the question, you are consciously letting that person know that you really want to know. It can be received as, you are not asking it as just a formal greeting, but you are asking because you truly care. The person answering the question still can decide how much they wish to share but, they may not automatically respond with "I'm good" anymore. The word "really", encourages them to think about how they are and the response they give.

Every day Mr. Justin would ask me the same question, consistently, and every day I would give the same answer.

One day, after the same routine of Q and A with Mr. Justin, I went home and started thinking. It has been almost a year, and this man has asked me how I was doing every day. He still greets me the same, his energy doesn't change based on my answer or mood, maybe he really does care. That night I decided, the next time Mr Justin asked me if I was good, I would tell him the truth. Why? Because Mr. Justin saw me. Like clockwork, when I entered the BGC, I went into the gym to hoop and on cue, Mr. Justin had walked in from the other side. He walked towards me, threw his hand out to give me dap, and asked me, "what's up Keem? You good?" I looked at the ground, looked back up at him and said "nah, not really". It was the first time I had ever removed my mask, let my guard down, and removed the distance between myself and an adult.

I didn't trust men, so this was groundbreaking. I said my youth development needed more, this was the beginning of those needs being met. I told Mr. Justin everything I could think of. How I was feeling, why I believed I felt that way, and other things like, how I was angry but don't feel like I can talk about it. The next thing Mr. Justin said was LIFE CHANGING! I was young and didn't quite understand it then, but I understand it now. He said, "Keem, there is nothing wrong with expressing yourself. There is nothing wrong with talking about your emotions and how you feel. There is nothing wrong with crying; crying makes you human, and we are all human."

**What**? A man of color. A MAN at that, just told me that it was okay to cry, that it was okay to talk about my emotions and what was causing me to feel a certain way, for the first time in my life I felt seen. It was the first time that I had ever heard a man speak of vulnerability in such a positive way, and in a way that did not take away from your masculinity.

There he was, challenging my way of thinking; challenging the lessons I learned from age 5 to 14, what it means to be a man, and in that lesson taught me that I can still be a man, be strong, brave, a protector and provider, while at the same time, be vulnerable, soft, strong, brave, a protector and provider. The seed was planted. I never forgot what Mr. Justin told me that day, and as I got older, it started to make sense. I don't always have to hide behind the mask. I am not crazy for feeling the way I feel, and actually wanting to talk about it. I learned, instead of putting on the mask in fear, to acknowledge the truth in that moment. If I need to keep information to myself, or, if I don't feel like talking about what is actually going on in that moment when asked, I can politely still say no, but also include, "I am not good, but right now isn't the time to talk about it, let me get back to you".

As much as I wanted to believe that this was a normal thing back in 2002/2003, society around me continued to tell me and show me that it wasn't. In the midst of me feeling like I was seen, I was quickly reminded that in this world, as a man, a black man, to be vulnerable still wasn't accepted. It makes you weak, they said, even though Mr. Justin told me it makes you strong. So I put my mask back on, and kept it pushing.

I do not have a degree as a therapist, but I understand the language of hurt; I can hear the sound of pain and recognize loneliness and depression in the voice. They say it takes one to know one; I wore my mask for 20 plus years, let's just say, I know what it looks like. I understand why we put it on, unfortunately.

Although you may not always be able to put yourself in someone else's shoes, you can always practice grace. You can always practice patience. You can always practice understanding, and as always, you should always practice love. To be seen, in some respect, for those who don't feel like they are seen, is to say without ever having to say it, I do care about you, and for some, it means more than you may ever know. I don't know when the last time you felt seen, but I see you.

# I Hear You

When I was in kindergarten, I had a speech learning curve. I stuttered so much, I could barely finish my sentences. I was often reminded of that. I tried so hard, again and again, over and over, whenever I attempted to speak, the-the-the harrrrrrrder it-it-it-it wa-wa-wa-was t-t-t-to fi-fi-finish. Whether at school or at home, this learning curve of mine was a turning point in my life.

In kindergarten, my teacher, a black woman, was kind, she was caring, and she was patient. She must have been teaching for over 30, maybe even 40 years. The gray in her hair proved her commitment to education. How she approached her job proved her love as an educator, and the mannerism with which she spoke proved her wisdom as one.

I told you earlier that I was very observant, the biggest reason for this was because I was also very silent. There's an old saying, listen more, talk less, how can you learn if all you do is talk? I was 5 years old, and before I ever heard of this saying, I was already practicing it.

Sometimes I feel like it was by choice, and sometimes I feel like it was by demand. I learned that it was definitely out of shame and most importantly, for my own protection. Being quiet all the time saved me from being bullied even more. It saved me from embarrassment-the fact that we are made to believe that something so natural as stuttering is embarrassing is a problem.

I remember my kindergarten peers calling me stupid, and asking questions like, "what's wrong with you?", as if the inability to complete a sentence was an indicator that something was wrong with me. Well, I started to believe it, there had to be something wrong with me because I was the only person who was doing it. I never met someone who stuttered growing up, so dare I say it, what was wrong with me, and why was I the only one. Have you ever tried talking to someone and in the midst of trying to get it out, flush out your thoughts, they give up listening because they don't understand you, or because you are "taking too long?" I can still see the kids, teenagers, and adults turning their heads mid-sentence to look away from me because I was not able to cleanly finish my sentences. To this day, there are young people who at a young age are shutting down verbally, which impacts them emotionally, which ultimately impacts them psychologically.

Educators, how many times do you find yourself trying to get answers from youth who are struggling with this? You pose questions in class, or even to them directly, and they don't display the confidence to verbally speak their mind and or share their opinion, how many times has this happened?

I remember family and adults saying things like, "hurry up and get it out", or "just say it already". In response, I decided not to say anything at all. I would spare you, and you, the trouble of ever having to sit through my stuttering again. I chose to never waste anyone's time again. I chose to protect myself, to do me and everyone around a favor, I chose silence. In the house, at school, in public places, I kept to myself, and stayed that way for a long time. As much as I wanted to talk, and as much as I wanted to say things, I didn't feel like I would be heard anyway.

I talked less, and listened more. This became my way of interacting with the world. I learned a lot this way, whether it was for good or bad, watching and observing everything and everyone around me gave me a superpower that I am forever grateful for. It gave me a set of skills that has helped me in life, as well as within the field of youth development.

Social cues and emotional intelligence are underrated skills that I believe deserve more attention in the conversation of what youth development looks or feels like. When those skills are strong, we as humans can interact with people in a healthier way, we can identify how to respond vs react, read the room better, and practice patience and understanding in a healthy way. When those skills are not as strong, reaction becomes the primary response vs responding, misunderstanding shows up, the wrong interpretation shows up, and all of these actions can lead to arguments and disputes.

On top of everything that was already happening, my household being silent, my decision to be silent outside the household, I was also in kindergarten struggling to read. I could not read, Kindergarten through 1st grade. Second grade I got better, but was still uncomfortable with talking or reading out loud. I understood all of the work though, I would watch and listen to how my teachers taught, and I would just replicate it on paper. I was great at being able to take what I just saw and listened to, and repeat it. This process helped me get good grades, and high marks on my test scores when I was younger. I just didn't know how to read.

I came home crying one day. I pulled out my homework, I was still in Kindergarten, and G-Money asked, "why are you crying?" I told her, "because I don't know how to read". Within a matter of days, G-Money came home with what was called Hooked on Phonics. She gave it to me as a gift. Every day I would come home and after my homework, I would have to spend time practicing my annunciations, syllables and grade level words. Hooked on Phonics was not a popular thing in the streets. To my peers, using Hooked on Phonics meant you were dumb. I used to listen to them crack jokes about it, say mean things about people who they either knew was on it or assumed was on it because their grades were not as high as theirs. The jokes about having to use Hooked on Phonics were ones I heard all throughout Elementary, Middle and some High School. I used it for a couple years, by 3rd grade I was much better, but did everything in my power not to let it be known that it was because of me being on Hooked on Phonics. Actually, this is the first time I will be sharing it on a large scale. I have never shared this with groups of people, and it wasn't until 2016, after Jeff told me to speak my truth, that I even shared it for the first time.

I'm older now, and I am grateful for the gift G-Money gave me. I would also say to anyone who is or will have to use Hooked on Phonics to practice and improve their literacy skills, there is nothing dumb, uncool or wrong with it. Using it for myself helped me slow down. I went from trying to hurry up and speak, to saying every syllable of each word when I spoke. I laugh now because I have had friends tell me in college and post college that I still do this to this day. I also learned that being behind academically doesn't mean you have to stay there, there is always room to grow.

Let me give you an example. I was working in schools as a teacher's assistant, an AmeriCorps member. It was a middle school, and I was working specifically with the 8th graders. I went to all their classes with them, supporting their learning and assisting the teacher in delivering the comprehension of the content. I loved it. By this age and time in my life, I had already known that working with young people was no longer just a job, but it was my social responsibility. I took this opportunity seriously, I saw it as a privilege and an honor to be an educator; and a part of a young person's development and journey. I went hard in the paint for my students.

On the first day of class, the teacher encouraged me to introduce myself, and without a second thought I did. As I looked around the room, and scanned everyone's faces, I saw a kid sitting in the back and locked eyes with him as I finished my introduction. He had beautiful dark black skin, his hair was curly up top, but not as curly as it may sound reading this, it was still low enough that if he wanted to get waves he probably could.

His eyes sat in his face like a crater on the Earth's surface, and he had a stern look on his face. The classroom had about 33 students in it and its diversity was beautiful.

After I finished my introduction, the young king called me over to his desk, he asked me, where are you from again, I told him Jersey, and this 8th grader told me straight up, get the fuck out of his face. Man! I laugh out loud every time I think of this moment. What a way to start the school year, and the beginning of what I told myself was a great challenge to accept. And so I did. I accepted the challenge, and I also got the fuck out of his face. I wasn't scared, but I knew that responding to him in that moment would not have made a difference, and reacting would not have helped. It was too early to respond, so I walked away and said to myself, I got you.

I watched youngin' for the rest of the class period, while he was in the halls transitioning to other classes, during lunch and afterschool. I paid attention to how he moved, how he talked, how he acted and who he didn't respond to. He definitely thought he was the big man on campus. The way he spoke to staff members, and his peers, told me he believed this was his territory, and that if I wanted in, I was going to have to work for it.

He did the bare minimum in class, and when he didn't want to do anything, he did nothing at all. He struggled academically, but I wasn't about to let him fail. I wasn't about to let any of my students fail, but this young king reminded me of me. He was an athlete out of school, he had a deep love for his grandmother, and academically he had already checked out. I knew why he was checked out, because I knew why I checked out, like so many young people who don't have the confidence in themselves to believe they can achieve high grades, what do we do, we check out.

I approached him as I approached all of my students, with love, patience, persistence, empathy and an 'I am here for you' attitude. This is just the foundation of tools I believe are helpful. I believe they are universal. You can be the smartest Math teacher in the school, the best organizer in the school, the best lesson planner in the school, but if your heart is not filled with these tools as the foundation, you are going to struggle to reach all of your kids, especially those who like me, gave up on school.

The most basic principle of being in the classroom, or in a youth space, is to love the young people who occupy it. If you don't or can't truly do that, being an educator is not for you, and you shouldn't be in their space of learning if you can't find it in yourself to embody and display that basic principle.

Of course, every young person should have their approach to what support looks like, and that I understood. I made sure that I had to learn what he needed and why outside of the foundation I always use. I had to learn what he needed and why. Every day I worked to get a little closer, and every day he would try to fight the urge to release his dominance. The first quarter of the school year was a chess match. I would encourage him to focus more in class, improve his attitude, and watch his mouth because he had one on him, but, in return, he would do his best to do the opposite. After the first quarter grades came out, he didn't do too well. To acknowledge students' efforts and academic success, even those who tried but missed out on honor roll by a couple points, I would purchase lunch for them. As promised, I paid for food to be delivered, and those invited came over to the table to eat. I remember talking about my grandmother, telling the students how much she meant to me. He was sitting fairly close to our table, so I am pretty sure he heard me, and something must have clicked for him, because things changed after that. As adults, as educators, some folx tend to believe, because they are the adult figure, and have to always be on point or very professional, they should never be real with their students and or share personal information. I disagree with that thought, depending on what is being shared. Young people don't always see the relevance or the connection between you and them because some folx don't provide that clarity. Me talking about my relationship with my grandma showed him I was human too, told him that we are actually more alike than different. I could have said to myself, don't share what I shared because it may come off as too personal, but instead I chose to show the human in me. He changed, we changed, our relationship changed.

He started cracking jokes on me, and his disses only told me that he was finally acknowledging that I was there. Regardless of him trying to be a class clown or prove that he was still the one running the show, he saw me and I saw him. I continued to invite him to study groups. I continued to have conversations with him, well, one sided conversations because he wasn't responding to much at first. I continued to give him the same energy I gave everyone else. Yes, he made me upset with the things he did, but I had to still love on him because I was finally breaking through. I needed to. If I stopped, he would have believed that I never cared, that he was right. But I did care, and I had to even on the difficult days.

Our relationship started to grow but his love for school was still stagnant. Another lesson I learned throughout my journey of being in this field of youth development, as you are being consistent, you also have to be persistent, and real with them. I had been asking this brother to come to my study sessions during lunch all the time, and he always turned me down. I get it, it's your lunch period, the only time you can truly be a kid, talk to your friends without being disciplined much, and you were free to go outside if you wanted to. Who would ever give up that freedom? It is a sacrifice, but I believed it was a sacrifice worth teaching the students I worked with. We have to put down the things we want to do, and pick up the things we need to do, in order to accomplish the things we desire to do. A couple days during the week, a small group of us would sit at the lunch table and review classwork and what we learned. We prepared for tests and quizzes that way. Sometimes I would bring in snacks that were not school related as a way to reward them for their sacrifice.

Young boy struggled in all his classes, but most definitely in Math. He wore his mask proudly. One day, the Math teacher said they were going to have a test at the end of the day. I invited the young king to study during lunch, I didn't ask him if he wanted to and I didn't make it mandatory. When lunch came, I sat down at the table and several other students did too. When he walked into the cafe, he walked over to us, looked at what we were doing and walked away. I could have stopped him, but I chose not to, just like he chose not to stay. Later that day, they had the test. I watched him squirm in his chair, throw his hands up, and show all types of frustration. He was the last person to turn his test in. When he did I pulled him to the side and said, "why didn't you come study? I gave you a chance to study and you chose to turn it down". The next thing he said brought me to tears. He said, "Mr. Akeem, I am in the 8th grade and I have never had anything over a 50 in Math, and for the first time all year he showed vulnerability and strength in the same light; he cried.

At that moment I thought to myself, how? How does a system push a student forward when they are not academically prepared? How does one get all the way to the 8th grade and no one checks his comprehension of basic skills? I already knew the answer to those questions though. Because I too was moved right along. It didn't hit me until I got to college, I was so underprepared in my College Math class, which was actually High School Math, that I was getting F after F after F on everything. Then there was the NCLB, No Child Left Behind Act.

I looked at the young brother and said "I hear you", your past is your past, but if you are willing to work for it then your future is yours to create, do not let your masculinity affect how your heart feels, now let's get to work". In that moment, without him ever having to say do you hear me, or are you listening, I heard him. He, like so many young people do on a daily basis, tells us they want to be heard. They show us, whether through temper tantrums, spicy attitude, or channeling their energy in ways that are disruptive to a classroom setting, they are telling us to listen. Something in us as educators have to make time to listen. The message isn't always straight forward, but it is in between the reason why they continue to stand up out of their chair, and the reason why they always want to leave the classroom. Do you hear them now?

The following Monday I asked him to meet me in the cafeteria to study for his Math test, he didn't respond, or even show an ounce of commitment and enthusiasm. I once again didn't force it, or make it mandatory by any means. I put the ball in his hands the week prior, that was my way of telling him that I saw him, and I heard him. I turned around and walked away. When the bell rung, I grabbed my things, spoke to the teacher and headed down to the cafe. When I walked in, I looked at the table and there he was, books open and ready to learn. We did this for four days. He would be in the cafe at the table with his books open by the time I arrived. We would go over all of the questions, and then I would ask him to do the questions by himself. Another lesson learned, I told him, practice doesn't make you perfect, practice makes you better. We would do the same question over and over until he could do it on his own.

That Friday, when the students took their Math test, he received a 60 out of 100. This may not be that big of a deal to some, and it wasn't to him, but to me it was everything. I have noticed that in my 19 years of working in the field of youth development, it is highly important to acknowledge the small victories just as important as it is to acknowledge the big ones. He came to me after receiving his test back, waving his hands, fluttering his body, and in a upset tone said, "see Mr. Akeem, I told you". I looked at him, and I asked him "are you serious?" Young King, you have never received anything over a 50 in Math but today you received a 60 and we only studied for four days. Just imagine if you studied every day, imagine if you studied before school during morning program, imagine if you studied after-school during afterschool programming, just imagine if your canvass was filled with confidence. Young King, just imagine, now let's get to work.

Over the remaining months this young brother met me in the cafeteria and we studied and we studied, and we studied some more. He started to receive 75's, 80's, 95's and 100's. He finished the school year averaging an 85 in Math. All I did was help him believe in himself. I reminded him, when no one else believes in you, you believe in you, now let's get to work. His grades started to improve in all his classes. He was taking more initiative to ask for help, to seek understanding, and to turn in his work on his own. He was self-regulating, finding purpose in his actions, and learning how to be independent. He was taking ownership of his own learning, a lesson I do my best to instill in young people.

By the end of the school year he was passing all his classes, his attitude improved, our relationship was strong, he was smiling more, showing signs of black joy, his confidence was high, and he finally felt heard. All that tough acting he did, was a sign that he was frustrated, not because he was a bad kid or a problem child, but because he wanted help but didn't know how to be vulnerable enough to say it. For the most part, his mask was removed, and he went on to graduate 8th grade, a feat he didn't believe in.

Oftentimes young people are placed in this bucket, labeled by their actions, and then some folx begin to interact with them based on what label has been placed upon them. How many of those who have been labeled, were pulled to the side by a community, a village of supporters and made aware that everything they are doing to be disruptive, to act out, is not who they really are. What positive messages were being sent to the young people? What conversations were being had on the individual level? When were they reminded that we do see them, we do hear them, and we will do whatever it takes to support them? I am not saying that it doesn't happen, I am saying that there are young people to this day who are still being labeled by school staff who have no idea what their home life is like, no idea what their social or mental balance is, and because of that, there is a misevaluation happening that is psychologically harming our young people. They are smart and they know the difference. Removing them from one class and placing them into another, much smaller class is going to get them questioning things. A lot of them begin to take on that persona just because they were labeled it, not because it is indeed who they truly are.

# I was Finally Heard

I started writing poetry in 8th grade. Correction, I wrote my first poem in 8th grade. It was a class assignment actually. The teacher gave us a choice, either we wrote a poem or an essay. The essay sounded too long for my liking, so I chose to do a poem because I could get away with turning in a shorter piece that would still be accepted. At the same time this assignment was given to us, Mother's Day was approaching. I didn't have any money to buy G-Money a gift so I decided that the poem would be my grade and my gift. When I wrote it, I started to share it with my friends. I was nervous because I had never been that vulnerable before, and I had never shared my emotions with G-Money. My friends were hyping me up, telling me that it was good and that I should give it to her.

I turned it in to my teacher. I remember him asking me about it, I told him it was for G-Money as a Mother's Day gift. I asked him, should I give it to her, he also said yes. At this point, the whole world was behind me so I had to give it to her. For me, this was an iconic moment because it was also in the 8th grade where I consciously made the decision to do better as a grandson. I had been getting in trouble, lying to her because I wanted to hang out with friends and in area's I knew she would have never approved of because of how long I was staying out.

Something hit me, a revelation of sorts, I started to acknowledge that I was tripping, and the attitude I was giving G-Money was uncalled for. She was not the reason why I was angry inside, so I asked myself why am I taking it out on her for no reason. Eighth grade was also the same year I made a commitment to never call a girl out of her name. To write this poem was everything, because in it I shared how I really felt about G.

I gave it to her on mother's day, and to my surprise, for the first time ever, I saw G-Money cry. I mean real tears y'all. She wasn't wedding sobbing, and dropping tears all over the place and out of control though. The tears came down slowly, one at a time, as if she was trying to hold them in, but every now and then would let one or two go. She said thank you, I responded you are welcome, and that was all there was to it. I sat there for a while, amazed, stunned, shocked, but at the same time in awe, because it was the first time I shared something that was truly on my heart and it had an impact on someone. But I was too young to embrace it, plus I didn't know anyone who wrote poetry, rap and freestyles were the kings of music and that is where I wanted to be. My friends and I would link up several days afterschool, when I didn't have sports and we would throw the cassette tapes into the Panasonic radio, grab our notebooks and pencils and begin to write raps.

We would buy instrumentals that already came on cassette tapes or we would buy a blank cassette tape, put it in one radio, play another radio that would play the song we liked, and record the sound. We also did that if we wanted whole songs as well. We would wait for long periods of time just to make sure we could record it. When the loop was back on, and the song was about to be replayed, if you missed it, it was over. You had to wait for the loop again, or try again tomorrow. I wrote raps all throughout 9th grade, into 10th grade. Prince Akeem was my rap name. Becoming the next rap superstar wasn't my goal, but I'm not going to lie, I thought I was nice; until rapping wasn't the same.

One day, per usual, we linked up afterschool and I started to try and write. I sat there for at least an hour and was not able to put together a single bar. I had another epiphany, all the things I was rapping about weren't true to me, and for some reason I started to struggle putting lines together. I remember going home, being upset, not at the fact I couldn't write raps, but I was upset at my father. I was upset at my grandad, and these emotions were pinned inside me for a long time but for whatever reason, I felt like I finally needed to get it out. I grabbed my notebook, and started to write a poem about the relationship or lack thereof I had with my granddad. The words started pouring out.

For the second time in my life I felt heard. It was also clear to me that rapping wasn't it, poetry gave me a freedom that was outside of sports. I introduced myself to the arts, and went on searching for ways to learn more about it. I wrote and I wrote, mostly stories in the form of poetry. I would listen to my friends talk about the things they were experiencing and write their stories in poems. I would write about life in general, along with things I experienced. I only shared them with my friends. I was shy, still had a stutter but not as bad, so reading in front of people was a no go for me. I was at the BGC one day when Mr. Justin introduced me to Ms. Alyson. The BGC was starting a poetry group and they wanted me to be a part of it.

I was the oldest in the group. I showed up, I participated but I wasn't all in just yet. Poetry was still just a side thing. After a couple weeks of meeting up and writing, Ms. Alyson told us that we had a special guest coming. She gave us an assignment, well a prompt to write about and told us to be ready when our guest came. When he came, I remember looking up at this black man, who was bursting out this jacket with broad shoulders and a small face. He didn't smile from the time he walked in, to the time he finished. Me being me, I ignored him as he was getting set up,  but when he spoke, I heard him. A big powerful message came from his stomach and out his mouth. I looked up so fast, and from the moment he started speaking he had my attention. He spoke fast, he spoke with aggression, as if he was still mad, still angry and in this moment was letting it all out. He moved his hands with emotion, as if pain was being taught in sign language. The whole building must have heard him, for a moment I swore he was only talking to me, as if it was only me and him in the building. He said his name was Shyst, Ms. Betty's Son, a poet from Philly.

He then went into a poem about being a fatherless child, and the emotions he felt throughout his childhood. This poem must have been written for me, because it was everything I felt throughout my childhood. Each line hit me, and hit me hard. By the end of his set AKA his performance, I said to myself, this is what I want to do. He is who I wanted to be like, poetry is how I wanted to inspire the world. I would speak it from my stomach, with a message just like him. I was only a Junior in

High School so I couldn't go see him perform in Philly because I wasn't old enough, but the impact was already made. I started writing more and more; every day I would practice my writing or work on a poem.

When I was Senior, Ms. Alyson told me that she wanted me to compete in what is called SLAM Poetry. I had never heard of it, I was interested until she told me what I had to do. It was a competition, and I had to stand on a stage in front of people to perform my poetry. In my heart I was like no, but I told her yes. I went through all my poems trying to decide which one I would say. It was only a one round competition because I could only remember one at the time. Watching Shyst perform his pieces without paper, straight from memory is how I wanted to share poetry. I practiced and practiced, every day for hours until I remembered it. The piece I chose was the one about my granddad and I.

The day of the competition, we drove to Camden New Jersey, and entered a building right behind the Rutgers Camden Campus across the street from the dorms. There were like 8 people in there, two of them were judges. I can't remember the other guy, but I remember the taller one, Vision. My opponent was a white kid who apparently had already been on the poetry and slam poetry scene. The way he moved, told me this was not his first time, and it wasn't. He went first. I sat next to Ms. Alyson, we both watched from the third row. When it was my turn, she told me to relax and do my best. My whole body was shaking, legit trembling.

This was a very personal piece, no one heard it prior to this day, and here I was, standing on this brown wooden stage, with large dark red like curtains behind me, bright lights over top of me, 7 people in front of me and one mic staring at me while I stared back at it. Still shaking I walked up to the mic, and began.

"This rope swung high, and every time that I tried
I just couldn't get it
This rope swung blind, and every time that I would try
I just couldn't get it…"

By the middle of the poem my hands moved with emotions as if I had learned to teach in sign language, 17 years of tears created a waterfall from my eyelids to the wooden floor. The message came from my stomach and out my mouth, still angry, still hurt, but in that moment I was letting it all come out.

When I finished, I cried while walking off the stage and into Ms. Alyson's arms. She held me, told me it was okay, and for the third time in my life I felt HEARD. When they announced the winner, my name was called. I was shocked and confused, but overall grateful. I walked over to the two judges, and Vision said, "keep writing young bul". Between Shyst, and this SLAM moment, it was written, poetry was my outlet to be heard. I continued to write, and when I turned 18, Ms. Alyson took me to my first ever open mic in Philly, the same place Ms. Betty's Son held his. I listened to old heads and younger cats bless the mic for hours. I was hooked, and fell in love with the art even more. I fell in love with writing.

The following group of poets showed me that this was a lifestyle, not just a hobby, it's a job for most, it's a culture and community that was embracive and inclusive. I studied it, and then learned that art comes with the responsibility of also telling the truth. I listened to Ms. Alyesha Wise talk about her love for her brother. I listened to Joshua Bennett and Alysia Harris talk about the perseverance of his mom, and she, the power of black women and women respectfully. Then  there was Just Greg Corbin, who stood on stages as a black man and talked about vulnerability and societal issues. Wow, I just heard vulnerability in poetry, and thought to myself, maybe they will hear me, too. My poetry transformed after that.

While in college, the little boy in me who was hurt, was still trying to be heard. Healing is a journey, it is a long process that isn't always determined by how fast you move. It takes time to address trauma, patience once you've done so and motivation to come out on the other side. I had held on to so much that even as a young adult I was still wearing the mask. The difference between my younger self and my order self at the time, was, now I knew there were spaces where I could release, the stage was one of them. However people weren't always a sure thing. I was still picking and choosing who I told what to.

The idea of me wanting to be heard wasn't a desire to be on a soapbox or to have a prestige level of popularity, it wasn't a look at me, listen to me mindset, all I wanted was to remove the mask. I didn't want to keep bottling up all these emotions and thoughts I had. I wanted to actually talk to someone, you know, the art of therapy.

I didn't even know what therapy or a therapist was back then, but that's all I wanted. While practicing my own self therapy I learned, bottling trauma while wearing the mask does more harm than good. Who was I actually protecting by keeping all this trauma to myself? Through self therapy, and the support of mentors who didn't know they were my sounding board, I started to open up more, both within my writing and in person. My life changed for the better. So when I met this young brother in Providence, I knew what was up, he was just like me and I was just like him. In that moment I had another opportunity, just like the people who made it their social responsibility to pour into me, I was about to make it my social responsibility to pour into him.

When I moved to Providence, Rhode Island, there was a level of excitement. A place I never been, opportunities in front of me, literally a new chapter. Couple months in, I was ready to go. Winter/seasonal depression is a real thing. I told my supervisor, Nick Figueroa at the time, if I don't start working with youth I'm leaving. If there's one thing I knew I needed in my life, it was the opportunity to work with young people.

I started looking into schools that welcomed afterschool programming. When I found one, I reached out and before I knew it I was back in action. After work two days a week, I was running my program. I took the same model I created while in Philly and implemented it here.

The first day of the program a group of students walked in, each had their own flair, but one young man was the life of the party.

48

He was loud, opinionated, funny, and attentive. Beautiful dark skin and a mini fro that made him look younger. His face was that of a young child, innocent, just like his peers. I introduced myself and shared with them my hopes for being an asset and a reliable supporter throughout their journey. I talked about my experience, where I was from, and then began to learn more about them. We played games to break the ice, and discussed what our community norms would be.

As time went on that year, I had the opportunity to see this brother in different settings. When I took the group to Washington D.C, who he was inside our program at the school, was exactly who he was outside of the school; except his energy was times 10. Up until that DC journey, he had been very quiet about his personal life. Again, having been in this situation before, both as him and as the educator, I understood why. We were still in the building stages. I wasn't sure how he took to men, or what his perspective of us were, but if it was like any of his peers, and the hundreds and thousands of young people who still practice this today, I am pretty sure he kept me at a distance. He only shared what he wanted to share, protecting himself in the process. I wasn't sure if he has had to deal with people coming and going in his life, but I understood the impact of that. I continued to move the way I moved, consistently removing one forcefield after another.

While on our way to D.C, there was an activity I did involving music, which helped me get to know young people better. The way it works is, they pick the song, and they break the song down. Sometimes I will give a theme and they have to pick a song that falls within that theme. The song he chose was a J Cole song, No Role Modelz. He chose several J Cole songs because J Cole is his favorite artist, but the first song spoke volumes. It told me exactly what this young King was feeling, and it told me how I needed to approach the relationship. The title itself was enough, but a big part of the song was him also talking about the lack of role models in his life. The song tells a story, and within a matter of 3 minutes and some change, this young brother was telling me his.

His Freshman year was a developing year, but one that had a lot of upside. He came to every session. Even when I moved the program from inside the school to out of school programming, he still showed up. He participated in everything we did but he was never the first to take initiative to do so. He had to be called on, encouraged. Tenth grade, he was showing signs of life, from a social and intellectual upside. Academics wasn't something he got excited for, so I had some work to do there, but I also knew that he needed more than just a pep talk about his school work, that wasn't going to catch his attention, talking about real life shit was. He saw himself as the man of the house, and felt as though he had a lot of responsibilities to take on. What are these Science questions going to do to help out my situation out at home? If the answer is nothing, then you need to come a lot harder with something that will.

I felt that. I accepted the challenge, and continued to focus on what he needed. Being a mentor, or running a program where there are multiple participants can at times be hard, especially when your own personal situation has challenges as well.

During his sophomore year, I had to lay G-Money to rest. It was and still is the hardest thing I ever had to do, accept, and experience. Being the human that I am, I found myself really struggling with this. I pushed forward, but I put the mask on to do so. I never took time out to process all of my emotions fully, because I was trying to keep it together, and run a program. All of what I taught to young people to do during these moments of vulnerability, I was now failing to do myself in 2018. That summer prior to 2019, I packed my schedule with so much busy work, that my interactions with participants were not the same. This must have had an impact on him; that and he was growing into his own now.

At the start of his Junior year I saw a difference in him. He was no longer the kid with all of the jokes, the biggest smile and the innocent look. There was a sag in his cheeks, a look of defeat, and I wondered, where did all his black boy joy go. He still showed up to most of our sessions but his energy had shifted. I was just getting back into the swing of things myself so I made sure to give him his space. As the year moved along I started to learn more about his feelings towards his dad, and his challenges outside of school. The pressure to perform was heavy on his shoulders. He was trying to live up to something, he said to me, "I am going to prove them all wrong", but never told me who they were.

In the midst of what felt like a young boy losing hope, society, particularly white America, was only making it worse. He, like many other black youth and youth of color had to experience violence and murder on a daily basis. It was on his phone, his friends phone, their tv's at home, in the news, and in their own community. Police brutality was being plastered everywhere, and the outcome of the victims weren't always positive. Murders and modern day lynchings; white violence against black and brown bodies can cause a lot of trauma. Young people had to walk around as if this was okay, had to go back to school, and for many of them, didn't even have an outlet to share what they felt. This brother walked around feeling like he was next, a target, and his feelings were valid.

The psychological and emotional impact of seeing such horrific incidents can really cause a lot of damage. His Junior year was damaging, but as a community we continued to lift each other up. He continued to wear the mask, and I continued to help him remove it. By the end of his Junior year, a breakthrough happened. Remember when I shared that as an educator, you have to keep it real with young people, well, one day after our session, I asked him to hang behind so we could rap with each other. We sat down and I started with a couple questions, just to remind him, that he is the one who holds the ball in his court, our relationship has not been what is has been because of a lack of effort on my part, so as men, let's talk about where we are, where you are, and what we both can do to be better, get better, finish strong.

He tried to deny it at first, telling me he was good, and that nothing was going on, you know, everything they will tell you just to get you to stop. But I wasn't about to let him win this battle, I cared too much about him. I then decided to take the lead. I told him how I felt about the last 3 years, about him as a person, our relationship and how much he matters. I reminded him that his life matters, his beautiful black life mattered. I revisited his own commitment, to prove them wrong, whoever they were, I told him, do it. "Do it because you can. Do it because you know what it means to you, but this I don't give a fuck attitude isn't it. And if you are going to prove them wrong, doing it this way isn't going to help". I told him, "I know everything outside of school isn't all good, that you feel hurt, that you have a lot on your plate, that you feel attacked, and don't feel safe all the time, but I need you to acknowledge those things yourself. When you do, the process, and the journey to healing can begin. I need you to confront what is going on inside of you. You have grown so much, you have persevered, you are already proving them wrong". I wrapped my arms around him and reminded him "I see you and I hear you, and I love you".

He finally got a lot off his chest that day. Of course he still had more, and a lot of work to do, but the steps he took that day were the most important ones. It reminded me of when I finally told Mr. Justin what was going on. I wanted to be heard. He wanted to be heard.

I don't know much about being a gardener, but if there is anything I learned about seeds, if you plant them, and you water them, they grow. That brother didn't need me to water his academics, he wanted me to support him, his understanding of life and how to grow in it. In education, there is this big emphasis on tests, teaching to the test, getting higher test scores, wanting to see students improve their academics; I get it, but I don't always agree with it. Test scores don't always prove how smart someone is. Getting straight A's doesn't always prove how resilient they are. But yet, in education there is this big halo placed on these markers as standards, which are supposed to result in high GPA outcomes, which leads to who gets into what College or University. Cool.

But not every student needs seeds planted to increase their academic ability, they already have it. I've sat in rooms with school representatives who would ask questions like, how do we build grit within the black and brown children who are showing up to school every day. The misunderstanding and lack of cultural competency lies within the question itself. A lot of black and brown children grow up having to be resilient already. Grit is on display every time they show up. As an educator, we need to understand what is stopping them from displaying this intelligence. Where do they need the most water, the most Tender Love and Care, how do they need to be seen and heard. When we figure that out, then we can water those seeds, and when we do, everything else will grow. I may not have paid attention in Science class as much as I should have, but that I do know. Before we label the seed, before we say what it can or cannot do, before we try to dictate what that seed will grow into, and or look like, learn to understand what is needed, and then from there water it, for it to grow.

# I Love You

The missing piece of my childhood development was social and emotional support. My grandparents did what any loving grandparent would; their best. With all my heart I truly believe that, and with all my heart, I truly believe that what I didn't receive was not their fault. If I never learn how to speak Latin, how can you expect me to teach it to you? As I got older, G-Money and I would have conversations about life and more specifically about her upbringing. She shared how she had to pick cotton in the field, how she tended to her brothers, dressing them up from head to toe. She talked about her mom, and how her childhood was very stern, disciplined, and busy. Every time we spoke, the picture was getting clearer and my understanding of what she knew was growing. She too, had never received the type of intimate support I was seeking as a child. It makes sense now.

My grandfather grew up fast, and took on a lot of household responsibilities at a young age. He put a lot of pressure on himself to take care and to support his family. When did he ever have time to receive social and emotional support from his folx? Healing is a journey, one that I have put a lot of energy into, even when it wasn't popular. Every day is another opportunity to take another step.

We are experiencing a state of emergency as it pertains to the mental and emotional health of young people, especially black youth and youth of color. I am calling it what it is, the type of attention this crisis requires, needs to come from everywhere. The financial support this emergency needs, must come from everywhere. We can't keep repeating this cycle. Lives are at stake, and every day we as a nation run the risk of losing more and more young people. The conversation surrounding Health and Wellness in our communities needs to continue to be amplified, addressed, and then supported. Therapists are essential workers in my opinion, and there needs to be an investment made in the field to help engage, recruit, and train more individuals who can also serve as representation in our communities.

We have to help young people understand that it is okay to seek help. We have to show them and tell them that it is okay to cry, crying makes you human, and that they too are human. We have to remind them that there is still strength in being vulnerable, that you can still be that strong person you want to be, and kind hearted enough to have feelings. There is nothing wrong with expressing yourself.

These types of messages have to become just as important during childhood development as trying to teach our kids Math. There is a young person sitting in their classroom  right now wearing the mask, this cycle has to be broken. I went 26 years without ever telling G-Money that I had a gun in my face, because that is how long it took me to finally put the mask down.

Our kids shouldn't have to wait 26 years to finally feel comfortable talking about the emotions they feel. Our kids shouldn't have to wait 26 years to finally feel comfortable enough to share that they identify as LGBQTIA; or 26 years to talk about the pain they felt, the sexual harrassment they experienced as a child.

We need to create spaces for them to know that they have feelings, emotions,how to identify them, how to talk about them, and how to manage them. In my 19 years of youth development, speaking and running my AkeemSpeaks workshops, the amount of young people I have listened to, and, heard from, told me personally that they have practiced self-harm, and have had failed attempts to suicide is heartbreaking. The amount of young people who have shared with me the things they are still going through is heartbreaking. I am talking about Middle School, High School and even College students who all have confided in me, as their attempt to finally remove the mask.

I documented these real life experiences, and if what I am about to share hurts you like it hurts me, I encourage you, please join the conversation surrounding mental and emotional health and help advocate for support and resources. Use your voice to bring light to the need that is hurting so many of our youth and adults. Push Health and Wellness as a positive activity to participate in. Bring attention to your Local and State Officials by talking about it more. Let us change the narrative and remove the mask one young person at a time.

Our contributions to the world is what changes it. I like to believe our stories are contributions to the world.

I tell them I see them because I don't know when they last felt seen. I tell them I hear them because I don't know when they last felt heard. I tell them I love them because I don't know when they last heard those words.

To every young person who has ever felt invisible, or still feels invisible, Fight back, I SEE YOU.

To every young person who has ever silenced themselves, or to this day still chooses to be silent, Fight back, speak, I HEAR YOU.

And to every young person who is still fighting, I LOVE YOU.

In loving memory of Madile 2002-2018: One is too many. Throughout my journey, and through my AkeemSpeaks, workshops, I have been given written testimonies from young people ages 12-21, sharing the challenges they were facing. Trigger warning, the next page are authentic notes that may conjure up past emotions.

I struggle with acceptance

I struggle with how to live and confidence. how to treat myself in ways others won't effect how I feel.

I struggle with loving others more than I love myself.

I struggle w/ expressing my feelings and talking to someone about it. With the ability to love my dad the same way I love my mom. Also w/ school academics.

Im struggling with.

· my self worth
· motivation
· procrastination
· indecisiveness
· not knowing who I am
· being too open / vulnerable
· rushing my own goals / success
· social anxiety (not knowing how to make friends)

I struggle when things hard for me.

I struggle when I s

I struggle w being scared t losing my lov ones.

Both of my grandfathers not see me gradu

telling my story

being vulnerable    crying

opening up

I Struggle    I struggle
with           with

Sadness
I struggle
with        Suicide
Fear

Depression
PTSD
Anxiety

death

I Struggle with...

. Self worth/self love...
. Loving Myself...
. Having...
. Daddy Issues...

Believing in myself, believing
that I can do it and succeed.

I Struggle with Loving    others
more than I love myself.

I struggle with my insecurities and
feeling loved by family

. Being homeless.

. Realizing my worth and believing in myself.

# We have to change the narrative on how we talk about healing, mental and emotional health

As cliche as the I can do it, you can do it too statement is there's validity to it. To every young person who will read this book, I was eight years old when I started having suicidal thoughts, and I was ten years old when I tried to take my own life.

The pain I felt growing up made me want to give up. But I didn't. I ultimately got help, started to heal, started to let people into my life who I believed really cared, started to put down the mask, and ultimately, started to live. All because I chose to fight back.

———————

Earlier I shared three actions that I didn't know much about, youth development, healing and self-love. That is not the same today. I have learned so much about youth development through my years of working alongside young people. I believe my experiences learning from youth have helped me build positive relationships with young people no matter where I am. And I'm still learning how to be better.

I started my healing journey as a Black man over 12 years ago. I didn't know I was healing then. Questions such as "why am I responding this way" and "why do I feel like this when..." drove me into a deeper understanding of myself that I didn't know existed. My answers revealed to me who I was deep down inside. Self-discovery became an interest. I wanted to learn more about myself. My answers were not always what I wanted to believe about myself, but the truth is, I had to face these truths. Running away from them wasn't going to make them go away; temporary relief wasn't going to help forever. This is the power of healing. You have to address what is there and take control of how you want to move forward. I began to let go of things I understood I didn't have control over. I began to talk about myself positively. I began to understand why I reacted to certain people and things vs responding. My life changed for the better.

Self-care was the most challenging action to learn. Although I have improved, it is a daily practice I still practice to ensure that I am implementing self-care practices. America is such a work reward-driven society that there was a feeling of always working towards the next accomplishment, even as a kid. Self-care can look different for everyone; as I got older, I started to expand my self-care activities.

Language is a powerful thing; growing up I had a love for basketball, and I still do, but there was something about basketball that made me feel happy. Consider a child who suddenly begins to show interest in painting, roller skating, or dancing; it is normal for adults to believe that their child is starting to identify 'hobbies'; and so we call them just that, hobbies. As adults, we will say, my kid loves playing soccer or learning how to play the piano. What if we identified their participation in those activities as self-care? What if the language we used to associate the things they enjoy doing defined self-care?

Self-care activities are essentially activities that bring you joy. They can be fun, relaxing, soothing, and give you peace of mind. Are the activities our young people choose to participate in bringing them joy? One could argue that they get attached to those activities because an adult decides to do yoga. What if we started giving our youth the language associated with positive mental and emotional health-related activities? What if I said to our six year old who loves coloring, "baby boy, I love that you love this self-care activity, coloring can be so peaceful right?" "What do you want to do today baby girl? You want to do another walk in the park and play catch? I know you do, because it's your favorite self-care activity. I love how you love to take care of your health".

At some point, they too will begin to associate the activities they love as healthy self-care options for when they need a break, when they are stressed or even depressed. This prepares our youth to be more aware and more conscious of their own needs sooner than later. As we provide them with the language to discuss and identify their needs, we also serve as the example and be readily accessible to have conversations with them about it. Or do our best to have educational resources available for that young person to tap into.

To every young person listening, it's not too late. You are still here for a reason. Through your challenges, you continue to rise. Even on the days you don't feel like getting up, you have, and I pray you continue to do so. I applaud you for not giving up even though you may have wanted to. I applaud you for not hurting yourself even though you wanted to. Today is the day you choose to fight back. Today is the day you choose to live, not just to exist. Today is the day you think about your dreams and begin to work towards them. Today is the day you let go of what you can't control. Today is the day you begin to love yourself. No matter who chooses to love you back, you love you back and give yourself whatever you need to love you. Today is the day you begin to have hope again, to believe again, to have faith that something greater is out there for you. Today is the day you choose to heal, practice self-care, and be the amazing human that you are.

I applaud you. You are seen. You are heard. You are loved. I don't know the last time you heard those words, but I know that you read them today. Read them as often as you need to, whenever you want to. Thank you for reading this book, your story will be one to remember, and I can't wait read about it.

I see you.
I hear you.
I love you.

Akeem Lloyd

Storytelling is a powerful and inspirational gift, it doesn't matter how old or young you are. Join our movement, share inspirational messages via social using the hashtag #MyStoryWill, and finish that sentence with something motivational that you hope to accomplish, or achieve. How will your story impact and change lives? Support the next generation, and help someone be seen. Please retweet, reshare, those stories which have inspired you through the hashtag. Let's uplift each other, so that others can be seen, be heard, and feel loved one story at a time.

#MyStoryWill be a source of infinite inspiration

#MyStoryWill remind them to fight back, to never give up, that their life matters, too.

#MyStoryWill will remind them they are beautiful, they are brave, and they are strong, no matter what

#MyStoryWill will remind them to try again, try harder, to try once more

To my Grandparents,

There will never be enough words that would righteously honor you both, because everything you did for me can't be summed up in a book. You took me in, raised me like your own, and for that reason I will forever be grateful. Watching you both over the years taught me so much, there's a lot of you in me that completes me. I honestly wouldn't change a thing, because every experience from the age 3 to 17 was meant to be exactly how it turned out. Because I was meant to be exactly who I am today. I miss y'all, I love y'all.

Granddad, you showed up for your loved ones every time, I watched how you always made sure those around you had what they needed. The lesson in that still resonates within me to this day. Thank you for teaching me; the value of family.

G-Money, my rock! The is never a day I don't think about you. You did everything under the sun to support us, to support me, and you always did it with grace. I work hard because of you. I haven't given up because of you. When they ask me why I do the most, I will tell them it is because of you. I love you. Thank you for teaching me; the value of community.

Love,
King

Please take care of yourself and call this number whenever you need help.

Suicide hotline 800-273-8255

Below are some websites there to support you.

https://therapyforblackgirls.com/
https://www.blacktherapistsrock.com/
nqttcn.com
soulaceapp.com
ayanatherapy.com
therapyforlatinx.com
therapyforqpoc.com
cliniciansofcolor.org
therapyforblackmen.org
therapythatliberates.com
lovelandfoundation.org
roottocrownhealing.com